UNCOVERING THE PAST:
ANALYZING PRIMARY SOURCES

BLACK TUESDAY AND THE GREAT DEPRESSION

NATALIE HYDE

Crabtree Publishing Company

www.crabtreebooks.com

Author: Natalie Hyde
Editor-in-Chief: Lionel Bender
Editor: Simon Adams
Proofreader: Laura Booth,
   Wendy Scavuzzo
Project coordinator: Kelly Spence
Design and photo research: Ben White
Production: Kim Richardson
**Production coordinator and
   prepress technician:** Ken Wright
Print coordinator: Margaret Amy Salter

Consultant: Amie Wright,
The New York Public Library

This book was produced for
Crabtree Publishing Company by
Bender Richardson White

Library and Archives Canada Cataloguing in Publication

Hyde, Natalie, 1963-, author
   Black Tuesday and the Great Depression / Natalie Hyde.

(Uncovering the past: analyzing primary sources)
Includes bibliographical references and index.
Issued in print and electronic formats.
ISBN 978-0-7787-1708-9 (bound).--
ISBN 978-0-7787-1721-8 (paperback).--
ISBN 978-1-4271-1682-6 (pdf).--ISBN 978-1-4271-1680-2 (html)

   1. Stock Market Crash, 1929--Juvenile literature. 2. Depressions--1929--Juvenile literature. 3. Stock Market Crash, 1929--Sources--Juvenile literature. 4. Depressions--1929--Sources--Juvenile literature. I. Title.

HB3717.1929H93 2015   j338.5'42   C2015-903236-9
                                            C2015-903237-7

Library of Congress Cataloging-in-Publication Data

Hyde, Natalie, 1963-
   Black Tuesday and the Great Depression / Natalie Hyde.
      pages cm. -- (Uncovering the past: analyzing primary sources)
   Includes bibliographical references and index.
   ISBN 978-0-7787-1708-9 (reinforced library binding) --
ISBN 978-0-7787-1721-8 (pbk.) -- ISBN 978-1-4271-1682-6
(electronic pdf) -- ISBN 978-1-4271-1680-2 (electronic html)
   1. United States--History--1933-1945--Juvenile literature. 2. Depressions--1929--United States--Juvenile literature. 3. United States--History--1919-1933--Juvenile literature. 4. United States--Economic conditions--1918-1945--Juvenile literature. 5. Economic history--1918-1945--Juvenile literature. 6. World politics--1933-1945--Juvenile literature. I. Title.

E806.H93 2015
330.973'0916--dc23
                                            2015017341

Crabtree Publishing Company

Printed in Canada/082015/BF20150630

www.crabtreebooks.com   1-800-387-7650

Published in Canada	Published in the United States	Published in the United Kingdom	Published in Australia
Crabtree Publishing	Crabtree Publishing	Crabtree Publishing	Crabtree Publishing
616 Welland Ave.	PMB 59051	Maritime House	3 Charles Street
St. Catharines, ON	350 Fifth Avenue, 59th Floor	Basin Road North, Hove	Coburg North
L2M 5V6	New York, NY 10118	BN41 1WR	VIC, 3058

UNCOVERING THE PAST

THE PAST COMES ALIVE

"Study the past if you would define the future."

Confucius, Chinese philosopher and teacher

Some events in our past have such a huge **impact** on our lives that they are remembered long after they occurred. One such event is known as Black Tuesday. Tuesday October 29, 1929, was the start of a **devastating** time in the world: the **Great Depression**. It was a time of loss—not only in the United States, but also around the world: lost money, lost jobs, lost homes, lost futures.

The past is any time gone by, from one minute to thousands of years. Looking back at things that have happened is an important step in understanding the **cultures** and **beliefs** of people who lived before us. Different types of **documents** and **images** help explain how and why events happened in our past.

Things that have happened in an area where we are help shape how we live. But things that happen in other places have an effect on us, too. Black Tuesday happened in the United States, but the problems that followed affected many parts of the world.

DEFINITIONS

We can define historical time in different ways:

A **decade** is a period of 10 years, a **century** 100 years, and a **millennium** 1,000 years.

A **generation** is all the people born and living at the same time, such as Generation X (1960 to 1980).

An **era** is a period of time with a certain **characteristic**, such as the Roaring Twenties (the 1920s).

An **age** is a very long period of time, such as the Stone Age.

▼ The first stock-market scare happened five days before Black Tuesday. On that Thursday frightened crowds gathered across the street from the New York Stock Exchange on the steps of the Sub-Treasury Building.

EVIDENCE RECORD CARD

Crowds on Black Thursday
LEVEL Primary source
MATERIAL Black-and-white photograph
LOCATION Sub-Treasury Building, New York City
DATE October 24, 1929
SOURCE The Granger Collection

HOW DO WE LEARN ABOUT OUR HISTORY?

We learn about our **history** by studying **evidence** of the past. This evidence is all around us. We can look at photographs and paintings, read documents and books and newspapers, or listen to speeches and interviews. Sometimes our history is passed along from generation to generation through stories, songs, and dance.

Historians are people who study the past. Many historians specialize in one era or age. Alan Brinkley is a historian who focuses on the Great Depression. He has written several textbooks that are used by students to understand how and why this event happened.

Source material about events can be found in many places such as museums, **archives**, libraries, and private collections. The stock-market crash and depression that followed were very public events that affected millions

▶ In the spring of 1936, Florence Thompson, her husband, and seven children traveled from place to place to find work picking crops. Florence often went without food to feed her children.

PERSPECTIVES

This photograph titled "Migrant Mother" has become a famous image of the Great Depression. What details in the picture tell you about what life was like for poor, **migrant** families?

"She said that they had been living on frozen vegetables from the surrounding fields, and birds that the children killed. She had just sold the tires from her car to buy food. There she sat in that lean-to tent with her children huddled around her . . ."

Dorothea Lange, photographer, about her photograph "Migrant Mother" of people. Thousands of records were created, as the media recorded the event in many ways: Reporters wrote daily articles in newspapers and magazines, government officials **drafted** new laws, and photographers documented the changes in people's lives. Because the effects of the depression were felt around the world, official records, letters, and photographs of the event exist in many countries.

One of the biggest collections of source material for Black Tuesday and the Great Depression can be found in the Library of Congress, which is the national library of the United States. It has more than 155 million items on file, including photographs, government documents, newspapers, maps, and audio files.

ANALYZE THIS

Are sculptures **primary sources**— why or why not? What do you think the artist was trying to convey in this sculpture?

▼ **This sculpture in Washington, DC, shows the despair of those waiting for food in breadlines. These lines often stretched across entire blocks.**

TYPES OF EVIDENCE

"It is impossible to write ancient history because we do not have enough sources, and impossible to write modern history because we have far too many."

Charles Pierre Péguy (1873–1914), French writer

Things that have been left behind by the past and give us information are called **sources**. Almost any way that people can record **impressions** or information—whether documents, images, or **artifacts**—are source materials. They can be created right at the moment of the event, or they can be produced a long time afterward.

These historical records give us snapshots of our history. They help us understand our past and can instill pride or horror at our actions. They can teach us what works in our society and what does not work, how we are the same and how we are quite different.

Sources are important and need to be **preserved**. Sometimes they are preserved in official ways such as in archives, museums, and public libraries. Other times, source material may be preserved by accident. This can happen when keepsakes or documents are forgotten in attics, or newspapers with historical articles are used to wrap old china or stuff walls as insulation. Private collectors may seek out and restore material on a certain time period or event to add to their collections.

▶ At a relief camp in western Canada on June 10, 1935, unemployed men got ready to board trains to head to the Parliament buildings in Ottawa. They were going to demand good jobs with decent wages.

ANALYZE THIS

Photographs can give us a lot of information about an event. Study this image. What do you think the conditions were like in this relief camp? What sort of people went there for help? How do you think they were feeling on that day?

PRIMARY SOURCES

Source material can be separated into primary and **secondary sources**. Primary sources are firsthand accounts or direct evidence of an event. They are usually produced close to the time that the event happened. Primary sources can be original documents or creative works that are written, **visual**, or **auditory**. They can also be artifacts.

Examples of primary written sources:

- Diaries and journals: Words written down about daily life
- Newspapers: Paper reporting on daily events in a certain area
- Blogs: Journals posted on the Internet
- Financial reports: Documents for businesses showing gains and losses
- Advertisements: A flyer or space in a newspaper to offer something for sale or rent
- Lyrics: The words of a song
- Letters: Correspondence on paper between two people
- Social media: Updates on social sites online

There are many primary sources about the stock-market crash and the Great Depression. During the weeks and months leading up to Black Tuesday, there

STAGE *BROADWAY* *SCRE*

VARIETY

PRIC 25

Published Weekly at 154 West 46th St., New York, N. Y., by Variety, Inc. Annual subscription, $10. Single copies, 25 cents.
Entered as second-class matter December 22, 1905, at the Post Office at New York, N. Y., under the Act of March 3, 1879.

VOL. XCVII. No. 3   NEW YORK, WEDNESDAY, OCTOBER 30, 1929   88

WALL ST. LAYS AN EG

Going Dumb Is Deadly to Hostess In Her Serious Dance Hall Profesh

DROP IN STOCKS ROPES SHOWMEN

Kidding Kissers in Talkers Burn Up Fans of Screen's Best L

▲ This headline is the most famous for Black Tuesday. *Variety* is an entertainment magazine. To "lay an egg" in show business means to fail in a big way.

"When the stock market went down to nothing there was people jumping out of two-story, three-story buildings in New York. That's what we heard anyway. Just jumping out! That was probably quite a bit of a shock."

Excerpt from an interview with LeRoy Hankel

were countless newspaper stories, magazine articles, and financial reports. The Great Depression lasted more than ten years. During that time, a lot of source material was created, including personal diaries, posters, and even "gold certificates," which represented gold held by the banks. A huge amount of primary source material was deposited in libraries and archives, preserving it for future generations.

ANALYZE THIS

Why is there so much primary source material about the stock-market crash and the Great Depression available for people to access and study today?

▲ Political cartoons in newspapers and magazines used humor to ask hard questions. This one by John McCutcheon in 1932 shows that even the economists lost their savings.

VISUAL INFORMATION

Primary source information can also be found in visual evidence. Since ancient times, humankind has been painting, sculpting, and carving. In modern times, still images and videos have added to our wealth of visual source material.

Images give us more than facts: They can bring out emotions. We can see the pain or joy in the faces of the subjects and get a real sense of the impact of an event. Before cameras were invented, artists captured people and scenes in paintings. This took a long time and cost a lot of money. Now we can preserve moments in history more completely and in depth through photographs and films.

Primary image sources can be:
- Paintings: Images made on canvas with paint
- Posters: Printed images with or without words
- Photographs: Images made with a camera
- Maps: Diagrams of a region or area

▼ From 1933 to 1944, President Roosevelt broadcast 30 "fireside chats" to the American people. In these broadcasts, he tried to explain his policies in a simple and direct way so that everyone knew what he was doing.

EVIDENCE RECORD CARD

President Franklin D. Roosevelt giving a "fireside chat"

LEVEL Primary source
MATERIAL Colored photograph
LOCATION The White House, Washington, D.C.
DATE 1938
SOURCE The Granger Collection

- Movies & videos: Moving images recorded by a camera
- Billboards: A large outdoor board showing advertisements
- Flyers & brochures: Small pamphlets with information about services or products

During the Great Depression, photographers such as Dorothea Lange gave us a **glimpse** of the difficult life of those people living through the loss of their farms, ruined crops, and dust storms. Her photos are held in an amazing collection of color and black-and-white photos from the Farm Security Administration in the Library of Congress.

Speeches, songs, and interviews are considered auditory sources. They are another way we can gather information about a historical event. Some of the most interesting primary audio sources for the stock-market crash are taped speeches given by the president of the United States.

Harburg and Gorney's 1930 song, "Brother, Can You Spare a Dime," tells the hard-luck story of a beggar who has lost his job. The lyrics of William Emberley's 1936 Newfoundland folk song, "Hard, Hard Times," describes how the depression affected rural life along the coast and the hardships many people felt.

ARTIFACTS AS PRIMARY EVIDENCE

Primary sources can also be objects or artifacts. Needlework, quilts, and feedsack dresses are some artifacts of the Great Depression. Other interesting artifacts are the clamshell "dollars" used in Pismo Beach, California, during the depression.

◀ Woody Guthrie (1912–1967) wrote many songs about the Great Depression, including the famous "This Land Is Your Land" in 1940.

SECONDARY SOURCES

Sometimes source materials are created long after an event and are not based on firsthand experience. These are called secondary sources.

Secondary sources can be:

- Novels & movies: Stories, which may be based on actual events
- Encyclopedias: A set of books that give concise information on different subjects
- Textbooks: Books used to give information on a topic
- Magazines: Publications that have articles written on a variety of topics
- Histories: Books about a certain time period in the past

How can you tell whether something is a secondary source? Read the document carefully and ask yourself these questions

- Does the author or creator get their information from someone else's work, instead of personal experience?
- Is the creator **interpreting** events or drawing conclusions, instead of giving facts?
- Is the date of the work long after the event, instead of closely matching the time of the event?

If the answer to any of these is "yes," then the material is likely a secondary source.

ANALYZE THIS

What can we learn about an event by reading secondary sources such as novels, newspapers, or magazine articles?

▶ In the movie *Modern Times* (1936), comedian Charlie Chaplin plays a tramp looking for work and trying to survive during the Great Depression.

Secondary sources can give background information and also let us see an event from another point of view. Sometimes we can see things more clearly when we are further away from an event and can see the big picture. This is called **perspective**. Historians can now see that the Great Depression affected many parts of the world and produced long-lasting changes.

Novels set during the Great Depression offer readers a glimpse into what life was like during such difficult times. John Steinbeck's 1939 *The Grapes of Wrath* tells the story of migrant farmers who face great hardship as they try to find a new life in California. *Roll of Thunder, Hear My Cry* by Mildred Taylor in 1976 describes the reality of facing racism in Mississippi in the 1930s, while *Bud, Not Buddy* by Christopher Curtis tells of a young boy trying to find his family during the Great Depression.

PERSPECTIVES

If you study the cover of the novel *The Grapes of Wrath*, or see the 1940 movie of the novel directed by John Ford, what would your impression be of life during the Great Depression?

▶ John Steinbeck wrote *The Grapes of Wrath* to shame those he felt were responsible for the Great Depression and its effects.

"Men and women huddled in their houses, and they tied handkerchiefs over their noses when they went out, and wore goggles to protect their eyes. When the night came again it was black night, for the stars could not pierce the dust to get down, and the window lights could not even spread beyond their own yards."

Excerpt from *The Grapes of Wrath* by John Steinbeck

INTERPRETATION

"The writing of history reflects the interests, predilections, and even prejudices of a given generation."

John Hope Franklin of the Organization of American Historians

When historians **analyze** sources, some sources are more valuable than others. Primary sources are made by someone who was a witness or participant in an event, so they are thought to be more **accurate**.

Some sources may be affected by **bias**. Bias is **prejudice** for or against one thing, person, or group when compared with others. Artists may show bias by putting a little bit of their feelings or beliefs into their work, while a camera makes accurate images of what is in the lens.

Historians use the three Bias Rules when looking at source material to recognize bias:

▉ Every piece of material must be looked at **critically.**
▉ The creator's point of view must be considered.
▉ Each piece should be compared with other sources.

During the Great Depression, people had strong opinions about the government and its role in the disaster. Many sources can be seen to slant in favor or against the presidents who ran the country at the beginning of the trouble, and the president who governed at the end. It has been difficult for historians to determine the exact cause of the stock-market crash because so many reports are biased.

▶ The French called the 1920s the "Crazy Years." People celebrated the end of World War I in 1918 with new fashions, new ideas, fun, and excitement.

JUDGING SOURCE MATERIAL

Bias is not the only thing that historians look for to figure out the value of source material. Other **factors** help them decide if a document, image, or artifact gives accurate information about our history.

In primary sources, historians use the "Time and Place" rule to judge the quality of the material. They believe that the closer in time and place the creation of the source was to an event in the past, the more reliable it will be. These sources can be organized from the most reliable to the least reliable:

- Direct traces of an event.
- Material created at the time the event happened.
- Material created after an event by firsthand witnesses or participants.
- Material created after an event by people who use interviews or evidence from the event.

Historians also keep in mind the **context** surrounding the creation of the source. Context is the setting in which the event occurred. The beliefs, customs, and world events at the time could change the way a creator portrayed the events in primary sources.

▼ As the effects of the Great Depression spread to Europe, people looked for new leadership. This poster to elect Adolf Hitler in Germany translates to "Our last hope."

"Little abandoned homes where people had drilled deep wells for the precious water, had set trees and vines, built reservoirs, and fenced in gardens,—with everything now walled in or half buried by banks of drifted soil,—told a painful story of loss and disappointment..."

Excerpt from *Letters from the Dust Bowl* by Caroline Henderson, June 30, 1935

The context of the stock-market crash and Black Tuesday was that it was a time of celebration and relief after the end of World War I (1914–1918). People had struggled and gone without for so long that they felt like spending without worrying about the future. This led to huge **debt** and risky **investments**. When the stock market crashed, this led to even bigger money problems for many people.

When looking at the struggles of farmers in the midwestern United States, we need to consider the context of the Dust Bowl. High temperatures, **drought**, and poor farming practices caused massive dust storms that ruined crops and destroyed the farms of people that were already losing their land and livelihood.

PERSPECTIVES

The context of this photograph is that it was taken during the years of the Dust Bowl. What does this image tell you about what it was like to live and farm there at that time?

▼ The dust storms that blew through Oklahoma in the 1930s were sometimes called "black blizzards."

THE GREAT DEPRESSION

"The country is not in good condition."

Former president Calvin Coolidge on January 20, 1931

The stock-market crash of 1929 and depression that followed changed the lives of millions of people in North America and throughout the world. It affected cities and farms, and both the rich and the poor. It altered the way banks and governments dealt with the **economy**.

The Great Depression left the United States in a mess: 12 million people were out of work, more than 20,000 companies went out of business, 1,616 banks went **bankrupt**, 1 farmer in 20 was evicted from his land, and 23,000 people committed suicide.

The hardships, despair, and poverty that people suffered changed the way a generation lived, worked, saved, and spent their money. For ten years, countries in North America and Europe battled high unemployment, failing banks and businesses, droughts, and **evictions**.

The Great Depression only ended when World War II began in 1939. Some historians say it played a part in the rise of Adolf Hitler from 1934 to 1945, as he gained the people's trust and turned Germany's economy around from its own depression. It led to Nazi Germany's military expansion across Europe and North Africa.

A wealth of photographs, documents, and artifacts gives us great insight into the struggles of thousands of people around the world.

▶ **The New York Times** has delivered "all the news that's fit to print" since 1851.

PERSPECTIVES

Imagine you picked up this newspaper on Friday, October 25, 1929—five days before Black Tuesday. Would the main headline reassure you that everything would be fine? Would you be nervous? Would you take action and withdraw your money from your bank?

ANALYZE THIS

The stock-market crash and the Great Depression had a massive impact on the population. In many cases, their impact lasted for more than ten years. List the ways they affected wealthy and poor people. Do you think these affects could have been avoided and, if so, how? What would you have done if you were running the country?

New York Times.

THE WEATHER
Cloudy and continued cold today; tomorrow fair and warmer.

Copyright, 1929, by The New York Times Company.

NEW YORK, FRIDAY, OCTOBER 25, 1929.

TWO CENTS In Greater New York | THREE CENTS Within 200 Miles | FOUR CENTS Elsewhere Except 7th and 8th Postal Zones

WORST STOCK CRASH STEMMED BY BANKS; 12,894,650-SHARE DAY SWAMPS MARKET; LEADERS CONFER, FIND CONDITIONS SOUND

Loud-Speaker Can Be Nuisance, McAdoo Advises Magistrates

The opinion that a radio loud-speaker, under certain conditions, may be classed as a nuisance was expressed by Chief Magistrate William McAdoo in a letter sent to the forty-six magistrates of the five boroughs yesterday. His letter declared:

"As you know, there is a widespread complaint all over the city by people who are annoyed and kept from sleeping by the loud-speaking radios in apartments, tenement houses and other buildings. Many complaints come to this office urging me to ask you gentlemen to treat these cases seriously.

"The person who starts a loud-speaker under conditions where it is found to annoy and disturb other people and keep them from proper rest, in my opinion, is guilty of a disorderly act, and where it is persistent and annoys a considerable number of people, he or she can be charged under Section 1,530 with maintaining a nuisance."

FINANCIERS EASE TENSION

Five Wall Street Bankers Hold Two Meetings at Morgan Office.

CALL BREAK 'TECHNICAL'

Lamont Lays It to 'Air Holes' —Says Low Prices Do Not Depict Situation Fairly.

FINDS MARGINS BEING MET

Sees Market 'Susceptible of Betterment'—Mitchell, Potter, Wiggin, Prosser at Talks.

Wall Street Optimistic After Stormy Day; Clerical Work May Force Holiday Tomorrow

Confidence in the soundness of the stock market structure, notwithstanding the upheaval of the last few days, was voiced last night by bankers and other financial leaders. Sentiment as expressed by the heads of some of the largest banking institutions and by industrial executives as well was distinctly cheerful and the feeling was general that the worst had been seen. Wall Street ended the day in an optimistic frame of mind.

The opinion of brokers was unanimous that the selling had got out of hand not because of any inherent weakness in the market but because the public had become alarmed over the steady liquidation of the last few weeks. Over their private wires these brokers counseled their customers against further thoughtless selling at sacrifice prices.

Charles E. Mitchell, chairman of the National City Bank, declared that fundamentals remained unimpaired after the declines of the last few days. "I am still of the opinion," he added, "that this reaction has badly overrun itself."

Lewis L. Pierson, chairman of the board of the Irving Trust Company, issued last night the following statement:

"Severe disturbances in the stock market are nothing new in American experience. The pendulum always swings widely and it would seem as though the long-expected break should bring about an equilibrium.

"The position of the Federal Reserve Bank is unusually strong and the borrowings of member banks are moderate.

"Considering the record-breaking earnings in many industries, we may well remember that whenever fundamental values are lost sight of by the unthinking majority it is time for courage on the part of those investors who have a real sense of basic worth."

Because the clerical facilities of brokerage houses are overtaxed as a result of the recent phenomenally heavy trading, an agitation was started yesterday in favor of a suspension of trading on the New York Stock Exchange tomorrow.

It is thought possible that the governing committee will take action today, without waiting for a petition from the membership. In many brokerage houses the pesting of books has fallen far behind and some relief will have to be afforded, according to brokers, unless the market quiets down shortly.

LOSSES RECOVERED IN PART

Upward Trend Starts With 200,000-Share Order for Steel.

TICKERS LAG FOUR HOURS

Thousands of Accounts Wiped Out, With Traders in Dark as to Events on Exchange.

SALES ON CURB 6,337,415

Prices on Markets in Other Cities Also Slump and Rally —Wheat Values Hard Hit.

The most disastrous decline in the biggest and broadest stock market of history rocked the financial district yesterday. In the very midst of the collapse five of the country's most influential bankers hurried to the office of J. P. Morgan & Co., and after a brief conference gave out word that they believe the foundations of the market to be sound, that the market smash has been caused by technical rather than fundamental considerations, and that many sound stocks are selling too low.

Suddenly the market turned about, on buying orders thrown into the pivotal issues, and before the final quotations were tapped out, four hours and eight minutes after the 3 o'clock bell, most stocks had recovered a measurable part of their losses.

Losses at Close Not Excessive.
The break was one of the widest

TESTIFIES HE HANDED $10,000 TO WARDER

Dell' Osso Asserts Former State Banking Head Counted Alleged Bribe in Home.

SENT BY FERRARI, HE SAYS

Memorandum on Withdrawal of Cash From City Trust Is Held From Jury Temporarily.

Gennaro Dell' Osso testified yesterday that he handed $10,000 "in large bills" to Frank H. Warder when the latter was State Superintendent of Banks. Dell' Osso, key witness for the State at Mr. Warder's trial for bribery, said he took the money to Mr. Warder's home for the late Francesco M. Ferrari, president of the City Trust Company.

The prosecutor presented evidence tracing the withdrawal of the money from the Atlantic Avenue branch of the City Trust Company in Brooklyn.

CHARLES E. MITCHELL, chairman of the National City Bank.
CHARLES E. MITCHELL, chairman of the Guaranty Trust Company.
WILLIAM POTTER, president of the Guaranty Trust Company.
SEWARD PROSSER, chairman of the Bankers Trust Company.
THOMAS W. LAMONT, senior partner of the Morgan firm.

Exclusive of the vast wealth of the

BIG DROP IN WHEAT; PIT IN A TURMOIL

Break of 12 Cents a Bushel to New Season Low and 8 Cent

TREASURY OFFICIALS BLAME SPECULATION

Drastic Market Decline Found Not Due to Any Action

BLACK TUESDAY AND THE GREAT DEPRESSION **21**

THE ROARING TWENTIES

The Roaring Twenties was the name given to the 1920s. With World War I just over, people felt it was a time of fun and **renewal**. After putting their lives on hold for so many years, people wanted to enjoy life.

For the first time people bought things on **credit**. The new way of thinking was to "buy now, pay later." Stores created **installment plans**, where people could buy something they couldn't really afford by paying a little each month.

People took out **loans** to buy houses and cars. They also used credit instead of cash to buy furniture, clothing, and vacations. This left many people in debt. They didn't worry, though; they believed they would always have a job to make payments. They didn't realize that everything could fall apart so quickly.

People's views about the stock market changed in the 1920s, too. Buying and selling **stocks** used to be something only the wealthy dared to do. But now ordinary people began to invest in stocks. **Stockbrokers** even found a way to let them buy stocks with money they didn't actually have. It was called buying on margin.

This new way of doing business was creating a dangerous situation. The September 25, 1929, issue of *The News-Palladium* newspaper had headlines that stock-market prices were struggling. *The World* newspaper reported on October 4 that there was worry about a possible sell-off of stocks. Most people ignored these warning signs that the bubble of spending and borrowing with no money was about to burst.

ANALYZE THIS

The 1920s are known as the Roaring Twenties. Why do you think they are called "Roaring"? What was special about that era?

▼ *The Great Gatsby* by F. Scott Fitzgerald was first published in 1925. It is considered to be the finest novel ever written about the Roaring Twenties.

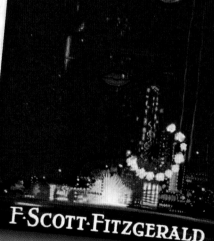

"At the news-stand she bought a copy of Town Tattle *and a moving-picture magazine, and in the station drug-store some cold cream and a small flask of perfume. Up-stairs, in the solemn echoing drive she let four taxicabs drive away before she selected a new one, lavender-colored with gray upholstery, and in this we slid out from the mass of the station into the glowing sunshine."*

Excerpt from *The Great Gatsby* by F. Scott Fitzgerald

VANITY FAIR

ONDÉ NAST PUBLICATIONS *Inc.*   35 cts · 3⁵⁰ a year

▲ This cover image from the December 1927 edition of *Vanity Fair* shows a group of dancers during the Roaring Twenties.

BLACK TUESDAY

The trouble started to show early in 1929. Throughout the year, stock prices fell dramatically then bounced back. By October, other signs **emerged**. Steel production was down, automobile sales stalled, and construction fell. Unemployment started to rise, as new goods flooded the market with no one to buy them.

Thursday, October 24, 1929, was the first big shock to the stock market. More than 12 million **shares** were traded. Panic set in. Banks and big companies tried to help settle things by buying huge blocks of shares. The next day, *The New York Times* reported that stockbrokers thought it was all brought on by **hysteria**. They believed everything would right itself again.

The stock market was closed over the weekend but on Monday, the market was in trouble again. Tuesday, October 29, was even worse: The market went into a free fall. People began trying to dump their holdings. More than 16 million stocks were sold that day, but no one was buying. By the end of the day, people had lost their life savings. Investors committed suicide by throwing themselves off buildings. It was chaos.

▲ *The New York Times* of Thursday, October 24, 1929, announces a steep decline in the price of shares during the previous day's trading on the New York Stock Exchange.

"The sum of it is, therefore, that we have gone through a crisis in the stock market, but for the first time in history the crisis has been isolated to the stock market itself. It has not extended into either the production activities of the country or the financial fabric of the country . . ."

Excerpt from a press conference by President Herbert Hoover, November 5, 1929

Shocked newspaper headlines the day after Black Tuesday read: "Wall St. in Panic as Stocks Crash" (*The Brooklyn Daily Eagle*), "Billions Lost in New Stock Crash" (*The Milwaukee Leader*), and "Wall Street Lays an Egg" (*Variety*).

People looked to the government for answers. On November 5, 1929, President Herbert Hoover gave a press conference. In it, he reassured the public that the problem was with the stock market and that the rest of the country was fine. Stockbrokers encouraged people to hurry and pick up the good deals on stocks now that the price was so low. Everyone thought things would recover quickly.

$100 WILL BUY THIS CAR MUST HAVE CASH LOST ALL ON THE STOCK MARKET

PERSPECTIVES

What details in this image tell you how bad the situation was after Black Tuesday?

▲ Walter Thornton of New York City lost a lot of money when the stock market crashed, and he was forced to sell his roadster for $100.

THE GREAT DEPRESSION

The stock-market crash threw the country into a depression that would last more than ten years.

In the first days after Black Tuesday, people were frightened. Even the banks were failing. Those who still had savings feared that their bank would go under and they would lose whatever money they had left. They raced to the banks to withdraw all their cash. Banks feared bank runs more than anything else. Some bank runs were started with just a rumor. If people heard a hint that a bank didn't have enough money, in a few hours, thousands of people would line the streets demanding their cash.

Jobs disappeared. With no money to buy items big or small, production in factories and companies came to a stop. In 1933, unemployment was at 25 percent—one out of every four people couldn't find work. There was no **welfare system** to help people, so they lost everything.

Herbert Hoover was the president at the time of the stock-market crash and the start of the Great Depression. People blamed him for all their problems. Families who had lost their homes lived in **shantytowns**, which they called "Hoovervilles." The homeless slept under newspapers, or "Hoover blankets," to keep warm. Few people could afford to keep or feed pigs on their farms, so they called the wild rabbits they hunted for food "Hoover hogs." There was no money to put gas in cars and people couldn't afford to fix them when they needed repairs. They got creative and hitched mules to broken-down cars and these earned the nickname "Hoover wagons."

▲ Houses in shantytowns were in such bad shape that they were condemned by officials, but people were so desperate that they lived in them anyway. One of the largest shantytowns was in Central Park, New York City.

"I remember crowds of people lined up outside (the bank), people were all lined up, snake like, hundreds of people. They were all out there, I couldn't see which way they were going.""

Walter Cook, a bank teller for the First Penny Savings Bank, South Philadelphia, 1931

PERSPECTIVES

Study the photograph below of the men in the soup kitchen. What clues in the picture let you know how they felt about eating there?

▼ In 1930, this soup kitchen in Canada provided food for unemployed workers. The food was basic, but it was often the only food these men would eat that day.

THE WORLDWIDE IMPACT

The Great Depression affected many countries because they did business together, buying and selling goods. Also, several countries tied the value of their money to the price of gold, and as its value dropped because of the stock market, so did their currency.

Canada suffered greatly through the depression, also known as the Dirty Thirties. Many of Canada's businesses relied on trade with other countries. As demand for their products and raw materials fell, so did the wealth of Canadians. Prairie farmers living in an area called Palliser's Triangle in southern Alberta and Saskatchewan suffered the same droughts that **plagued** the midwestern United States. This area also became a Dust Bowl and Canadian farmers lost their crops to dust storms, hailstorms, and swarms of insects.

Unemployment in Canada was even higher than the United States: 30 percent of Canadians were out of work by 1933. Overseas, the highest unemployment

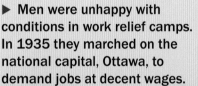

▶ Men were unhappy with conditions in work relief camps. In 1935 they marched on the national capital, Ottawa, to demand jobs at decent wages.

"Dear Sir Henry–

"To-day I am writing you these couple of line to ask you a great favor. Because it's a week that I have been not able to go to school because I have no shoes. Will you will really say that I am a great pest but I am really writing in crying to see that here we have so much trouble with relief while other in other place have no trouble."

Letter to Premier George S. Henry of Ontario, February 25, 1933

was in northern England, where rates went up to 70 percent in some towns.

The situation in Germany was **dire**. The government there had borrowed money from the United States, and as the depression hit, American banks called in their loans. Germany could not afford to pay back the money. Its economy came to a standstill. More than six million people were out of work and many people were starving to death.

The German people were unhappy with their government. They decided to vote for a new chancellor who promised to turn things around. He put people back to work building a vast highway system called the autobahn. German factories made all the materials they needed for the project. People thought he was a great leader. His name was Adolf Hitler, and the Great Depression helped bring him to power.

▼ At one point, German banknotes became so worthless that people used them as wallpaper.

REICHSBANKNOTE

Eine Million Mark

zahlt die Reichshauptkasse in Berlin gegen diese Banknote dem Einlieferer

Berlin, den 20 Februar 1923

Reichsbankdirektorium

Mark 1.000.000 Mark

▲ In 1936, unemployed shipworkers marched from Jarrow in the north of England south to London to demand work. Their "hunger march" helped create awareness of their problems.

ANALYZE THIS

Why was it so important to help American farmers during the New Deal? Why had they suffered so badly?

THE NEW DEAL

In October 1932, President Herbert Hoover gave a speech in which he stated that "the tide has turned and that the gigantic forces of depression are today in retreat." But it was not so. Things were as bad as ever. People wanted new leadership. In November 1932, Franklin D. Roosevelt (F. D. R.) was voted in as the new president.

By studying F. D. R.'s **inauguration** speech, we can see that he was very direct about the problems facing the country but also confident and optimistic that things could be fixed. He encouraged the public to not be afraid to invest again: "The only thing we have to fear is fear itself." He also outlined his plans for getting the economy back on track: "Our greatest primary task is to put people to work."

F. D. R.'s plan to accomplish this was called the **New Deal**. In it, unemployed young men were given jobs working on building projects such as new bridges, buildings, and roads. F. D. R. also believed that by helping farmers first, the economy would recover.

The problems of the Great Depression made people aware of how **vulnerable** people were when things went wrong. In August 1935, F. D. R.

A MULE AND A PLOW

RESETTLEMENT ADMINISTRATION
Small Loans Give Farmers a New Start

▲ The Resettlement Administration gave small loans to farmers to get them back on their feet.

"*Most of the farmers, just about all of them, when the WPA came in, worked on the roads. I think, as I remember, they got a dollar a day for working. And if they had a team of horses, they got an extra 50 cents a day for the horses.*"

Excerpt from an interview with Stan Jensen about the Works Progress Administration of the New Deal

signed the Social Security Act into law. This new law helped provide basic necessities for the poor. It also created a social insurance program to pay retired workers aged 65 or older. In his speech while signing the new act, he said, "We can never insure one hundred percent of the population against one hundred percent of the hazards and **vicissitudes** of life, but we have tried to frame a law that will give some measure of protection to the average citizen and to his family against the loss of a job and against poverty-ridden old age."

▼ The National Recovery Administration brought business, labor, and workers together to work out fair work practices and wages.

▼ This political cartoon of 1935 shows President Roosevelt surrounded by his New Deal agencies.

PERSPECTIVES

What details in this cartoon show how the illustrator felt about Roosevelt's New Deal agencies? Was he teasing Roosevelt?

DEPTHS OF DEPRESSION

"People caught in their own yards grope for the doorstep. Cars come to a standstill, for no light in the world can penetrate that swirling murk . . ."

Avis D. Carlson writing in the *New Republic*

PERSPECTIVES

What sort of feelings do you get about the workers in this painted mural? Does the mural portray New Deal jobs as good things or as bad things?

In the big cities, most people didn't have money to feed themselves or their families. Every town or community had a soup kitchen. At first soup kitchens were run by churches or charities either outdoors, or in church halls, or in cafeterias. As the depression worsened, the government stepped in to set up more.

Many people were upset at losing their jobs. They joined unions to protect their jobs and wages. Unions became stronger thanks to laws that gave them **bargaining** power.

Gradually, changes began to occur that helped people through the Great Depression. The Works Progress Administration (WPA) was a New Deal program. It employed millions of people to construct roads, parks, and schools. One special project—called Project Number One—paid artists, writers, actors, and musicians to create works of art.

At the beginning of the Great Depression, almost all city residents had electricity, but only about ten percent of farmers did. The Rural Electrification Act of 1935 brought electricity to rural areas for the first time. Photographs show men working together to raise tall poles to hold the wires. It was very exciting for many farm families the "day the lights went on." Unfortunately, very few farmers could afford to buy new electric appliances.

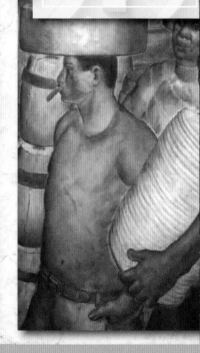

▲ Charles Wells's mural shows workers taking on difficult and dirty jobs to make money to support themselves and their families.

▶ Exhibitions of paintings and other works of art were held across the United States, largely paid for by the WPA Federal Art Project Number One.

EXHIBITION
OF
OIL PAINTINGS
BY ARTISTS IN THE EASEL DIVISION OF THE
W.P.A. FEDERAL ART PROJECT
AT THE W.P.A. FEDERAL ART PROJECT GALLERY
7 EAST 38th STREET
FEB. 23 TO MAR. 23
GALLERY OPEN DAILY EXCEPT SUNDAY-12 M-5 P.M.

EVIDENCE RECORD CARD

"New Deal" by Charles Wells
LEVEL Primary source
MATERIAL Painted mural
LOCATION Clarkson S. Fisher
Federal Building and U.S.
Courthouse, Trenton, New Jersey
DATE 1935
SOURCE Library of Congress

ANALYZE THIS

Do you think that the penny auctions were a good idea for the farmers? And what about for the banks?

A BATTLE FOR SURVIVAL

Banks were failing in record numbers. In the first ten months of the Great Depression, 744 banks went bankrupt. After that, about 70 failed per year. With people withdrawing what was left of their savings in record numbers, banks were low on cash. Many people fell behind on their loan or mortgage payments. The banks responded by **foreclosing** on properties and seizing goods.

Farmers were caught in a desperate situation. The years of drought and the dust storms had destroyed their farmland. Those living in the Dust Bowl couldn't grow anything. Those that could harvest crops found no one to buy them and therefore had no **income**. They couldn't find the money for their payments.

When the banks foreclosed, farmers not only lost homes, they also lost their livelihoods. The bank often **auctioned** off the property, livestock, and furniture. As more and more people lost everything, their friends and neighbors saw the banks as evil. They came up with a way to help. They attended the auctions and would only bid one penny. No one else would up the bid. The bank had to sell and lost money.

"I don't know why we got it. It was some tractor, anyways, an Allis-Chalmers. It was the hardest thing to drive. I went out to disc or harrow with it. I think I took out about half the fence. It wouldn't stop when I said, 'Whoa!'"

Excerpt from an interview with Helen Bolton

▲The Hoover Dam was built at the height of the Great Depression. The project employed more than 21,000 men, including these painters.

The banks turned to the government for help. The government put a halt to foreclosures for a year.

Farmers who were dealing with the Dust Bowl looked for new land somewhere else. Advertisements made California sound like the perfect place to farm. Thousands migrated west along Route 66 to start over.

▶ The theater production *Machine Age* was the product of another WPA project. Singing, acting, and dancing acts were performed in this musical comedy.

W.P.A. FEDERAL THEATRE PRESENTS

MACHINE AGE

A VARIETY THEATRE PRODUCTION

A NEW MUSICAL COMEDY BY WILLIAM SULLY .... Music by Bert Reed

MAJESTIC THEATRE FULTON ST. AND ASHLAND PL. BROOKLYN

▶ Panic spread as banks closed. In towns where one bank failed, people would rush to their own bank to withdraw money, causing it to fail as well.

HISTORY REPEATED

"Unemployment is sky-rocketing; deflation is in our future for the first time since the Great Depression. I don't care whose fault it is, it's the truth."

John Mellencamp, American rock singer

There have been other recessions and depressions since the 1930s. Officials use the term "depression" with caution. It has a more negative meaning than the word "recession."

Both terms refer to a **downturn** in the economy, but different words have different effects on people. If people are afraid for the safety of their savings, jobs, or homes, they will act to protect them. When thousands of people withdraw money or cut back on spending, the economy can suffer even if there isn't a recession or depression. A time of bank runs and big withdrawals during these times are called "panics." There were eight "panics" from 1785 to the Great Depression. Since 1929, the world has experienced more than ten recessions, some worse than others.

Government graphs are nice visual explanations of the drop in construction, unemployment rates, and real estate prices. Political cartoons point the finger of blame and poke fun at the government. Reading through them gives the reader a glimpse into changing ideas and opinions about the causes of, and solutions to, the problem.

Photographs let us see the reaction, the public has to recessions. Sometimes the images show us people who are devastated and hopeless, and other times we see anger and protest.

In 2011, thousands of people marched down Wall Street in New York in a protest about the imbalance of wealth in the United States. The Occupy Wall Street movement continued for several years and spread to other countries.

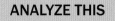

ANALYZE THIS

Would it be better or worse for the economy if economists didn't label downturns as a "depression"?

RECENT TIMES

Many people around the world were affected by a recession in 2007 and 2008. It was called the worst recession since the Great Depression. It started with the sudden decrease in housing prices in the United States. Once this "housing bubble" burst, the economy quickly slipped into a recession.

Just like during the Great Depression, many people lost their homes when the banks foreclosed on their properties. Although in the 1930s it was mostly farms, it was houses in towns and cities in 2007. From 2007 to 2011, more than four million families lost their homes. Entire neighborhoods became ghost towns.

Because of the memories of the Great Depression, banks and the government reacted quickly to try to stop the slide in the economy. The American Recovery and Reinvestment Act (ARRA) was signed

▶ Detroit, Michigan was one of the hardest-hit cities for foreclosures during the recession. By 2009 more than 70,000 foreclosures had already taken place.

"I know what it's like to be homeless and to not have a home, and have children in the street living from place to place. It's horrible, it's horrible."

Regina Moore, Detroit, Michigan

PERSPECTIVES

What statement does this 2009 photograph of a shack near the headquarters of the automobile maker, General Motors, make about the sharing of wealth in the country?

into law on February 17, 2009 by President Barack Obama. The main focus of the ARRA was to save and create jobs. It also gave relief payments to those people hardest hit by the recession and helped with healthcare for those who couldn't afford it. The act also encouraged investments in science, transportation, education, and the environment. With the help of the ARRA, the recession in the United States did not go as deep or last as long as the Great Depression.

With modern **technology**, such as digital records, and public Internet access, primary sources, such as a **transcript** of the ARRA, can be viewed by anyone.

ANALYZE THIS

Did the officials' reaction to the 2007 recession show that the government had learned anything from the Great Depression?

▲ Many foreclosed homes are still vacant. Residents are worried that empty houses and neighborhoods will attract crime to their area.

MODERN EXAMPLES

THE WORLDWIDE IMPACT

The effects of the recession in the United States in 2007 soon spread to Europe. With banks and businesses linked across borders, problems in one country can often cause problems in others. Europe soon also struggled with a recession.

When European banks started to fail, governments **bailed** them out with public money. This caused huge debts for countries. Greece faced one of the biggest debts and the **Eurozone** countries had to lend it money to pay its bills. To receive the money, Greece had to introduce strong **austerity measures**. The Country had to reduce its spending, cut pensions and benefits, and increase taxes to bring in more money.

The Greek public responded to the austerity measures with anger. On May 5, 2010, they held a massive national strike to protest pay cuts, higher taxes, and layoffs. In the capital city of Athens, the strike turned violent: Three people were killed, many were seriously injured or hurt, and more than 100 people were arrested.

Other countries in Europe felt the effects of what was being called "The Great Recession," too. Unemployment rates went up sharply in Italy, Ireland, Portugal, Spain, and the United Kingdom. Countries had to introduce new policies to help their economies through troubled times.

"The focus of the presidency . . . is clear: We need to finish what we started; we need to deliver as much of our growth and jobs agenda as we possibly can."
José Manuel Barroso, president of the European Commission, speaking in January 2014

▲ World leaders met regularly to discuss the economic crisis and how they might solve it. This meeting took place at Davos in Switzerland in 2015.

WORLD ECONOMIC FORUM

COMMITTED TO IMPROVING THE STATE OF THE WORLD

▼ Thousands of people took to the streets of Thessaloniki in Greece in September 2012 to protest tax hikes and wage cuts.

The slogans on the protestors' signs included:

▪ I vote, You vote, He votes, We vote, You vote, They steal.

▪ We do not owe, we will not sell away, we will not pay.

TIMELINE

1918

November 11, 1918 World War I ends

1920–1929 The Roaring Twenties, a time of spending

March 4, 1929 Herbert Hoover takes office as president of the United States

March 25, 1929 Mini-crash of the stock market, showing early signs of trouble

September 3, 1929 Stock market reaches its peak

October 24, 1929 Black Thursday: Stock prices drop, but banks prop up the market

October 29, 1929 Black Tuesday: Stock market crashes as 16.4 million shares are traded

October 30, 1929 Start of the Great Depression

Summer 1931 First "penny auction" at the Von Bonn family farm in Nebraska

1933

January 30, 1933 Adolf Hitler becomes chancellor of Germany

March 4, 1933 Franklin D. Roosevelt takes office as president

March 1933 Leiter's Pharmacy in Pismo Beach, California, issues clamshell money during F. D. R.'s bank holiday

March 12, 1933 F. D. R.'s first "fireside chat"

July 1933 The Public Works Administration (PWA) begins putting people to work on projects such as bridges, hospitals, and schools

April 3, 1935 The Works Progress Administration (WPA), a New Deal agency, puts unemployed people to work building roads and public buildings

August 1935 The Social Security Act is signed, providing money for senior citizens

1935

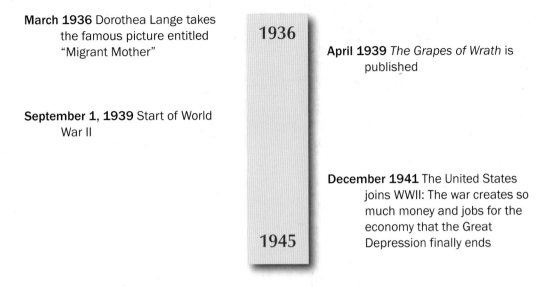

March 1936 Dorothea Lange takes the famous picture entitled "Migrant Mother"

1936

April 1939 *The Grapes of Wrath* is published

September 1, 1939 Start of World War II

December 1941 The United States joins WWII: The war creates so much money and jobs for the economy that the Great Depression finally ends

1945

Average percentage of the labor force unemployed during the Great Depression.

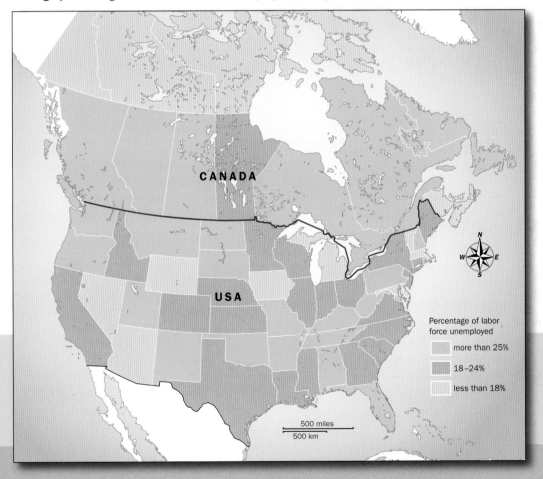

CANADA

USA

Percentage of labor force unemployed

more than 25%

18–24%

less than 18%

500 miles

500 km

BIBLIOGRAPHY

CHAPTER OPENER QUOTATIONS

p.4 Confucius: *The Analects of Confucius: A New Millenium Translation.* Premier Pub Co, 1999.

p.8 Charles Pierre Péguy: *Clio,* 1931.

p.16 John Hope Franklin: *African-American Biography,* Vol. 2, 1994.

p.20 Calvin Coolidge: *The Spokesman Review,* January 21, 1931.

p.32 Avis D. Carlson article, *New Republic,* April 1935.

p.36 John Mellencamp: www.quotessays.com/john-mellencamp.html

EXCERPTS

p.6 Lange, Dorothea. *Popular Photography,* February 1960.

p.10 Hankel, LeRoy. Audio interview: www.livinghistoryfarm.org

p.15 Steinbeck, John. *The Grapes of Wrath.* Penguin Classics, 2006.

p.18 Henderson, Caroline. *The Atlantic,* May 1936.

p.22 Fitzgerald, F. Scott. *The Great Gatsby,* Scribner, 2004.

p.24 Hoover, Herbert. Press conference, November 5, 1929.

p.26 Cook, Walter. "Closed for Business," Historical Society of Pennsylvania.

p.28 Letter to Premier George S. Henry of Ontario, February 25, 1933. Archives of Ontario, ref. code: RG 3-9-0-391.

p.30 Hoover, Herbert. Address at the Coliseum in Des Moines, Iowa, October 4, 1932.

p.30 Jensen, Stan. Audio interview: www.livinghistoryfarm.org

p.34 Bolton, Helen. Audio interview: www.livinghistoryfarm.org

p.38 Moore, Regina. Fox 2 News transcript for February 10, 2015: www.myfoxdetroit.com

p.40 President Barroso. European Commission press release database: Speech, Strasbourg, January 15, 2014.

TO FIND OUT MORE

Non-Fiction Books:
Freedman, Russell. *Children of the Great Depression.* Clarion Books, 2010.

Mullenbach, Cheryl. *The Great Depression for Kids: Hardship and Hope in 1930s America.* Chicago Review Press, 2015.

Stanley, Jerry. *Children of the Dust Bowl.* Crown Publishers, 1993.

Historical Fiction:
Curtis, Christopher Paul. *Bud, Not Buddy.* Laurel Leaf, 2004.

Morck, Irene. *Five Pennies: A Prairie Boy's Story,* Fifth House, 1999.

Peck, Richard. *A Year Down Yonder,* Puffin, 2002.

Taylor, Cora. *Summer of the Mad Monk.* Greystone Books, 1994.

Taylor, Mildred D. *Roll of Thunder, Hear My Cry.* Puffin Books, 2004.

INTERNET GUIDELINES

Finding good source material on the Internet can sometimes be a challenge. When analyzing how reliable the information is, consider these points:

- Who is the author of the page? Is it an expert in the field or a person who experienced the event?
- Is the site well known and up to date? A page that has not been updated for several years probably has out-of-date information.
- Can you verify the facts with another site? Always double-check information.

- Have you checked all possible sites? Don't just look on the first page a search engine provides. Remember to try government sites and research papers.
- Have you recorded website addresses and names? Keep this data so you can backtrack and verify the information you want to use.

MULTIMEDIA
Children of the Great Depression video shows what the 1930s were like for children:
www.youtube.com/watch?v=WtUjpUW09qc&spfreload=10

WEBSITES:
Living History Farm gives great insight into farming during the Great Depression, including audio interviews:
www.livinghistoryfarm.org/farmingin the30s/money_01.html

Kidskonnect has many interesting facts, as well as many links to other websites:
https://kidskonnect.com/history/great-depression

PBS Kids looks at the stock-market crash and the Great Depression:
www.pbs.org/wnet/newyork//laic/episode6/topic1/e6_topic1.html

42 Explore offers great links to informational websites, as well as fun activities:
www.42explore2.com/depresn.htm

GLOSSARY

accurate Correct in all details

age A distinct period of history

analyze Examine closely

archives A place where a collection of historical documents is stored

artifacts Objects made by human beings

auction A public sale

auditory Of or relating to things that can be heard

austerity measures Official actions taken by a government to reduce the money it owes

bailed To pay money to help out

bankrupt Unable to pay one's debts

bargaining Dealing and trading

beliefs Things accepted as truths

bias Prejudice in favor of or against one thing, person, or group

century 100 years

context The circumstances or setting in which an event happens

credit An account that is paid later

critically Seriously and carefully

culture The arts and other achievements of a society

debt Money owed

decade A period of ten years

devastating Very distressing

dire Extremely serious

document A piece of paper that provides an official record of something

downturn A decline in business

drafted Prepared a first version of something

drought A long period of no rain

economists Experts on how money is earned and spent in society

economy The wealth and resources of a country

emerged Came out

era A period of history with a distinct characteristic

Eurozone The 19 countries of the European Union that share the Euro as their common currency

eviction Being forced out of a home

evidence The body of facts or information to show whether something is true

factors Facts that contribute to a result

foreclosing Taking possession of a property

generation All the people born and living at the same time

glimpse A brief or partial view

Great Depression, the The economic crisis that began in 1929 and ended during World War II

historian A person who uses evidence to determine what happened in the past

history Past events and their description

hysteria Wild emotions

image A visual likeness of someone or something in a painting, photo, or film

impact A strong effect

impressions Images

inauguration The beginning of someone's time in government

income Money received during a given period as wages for work done

installment plan Payment plan by which people paid for something in small monthly payments

interpreting Explaining the meaning of something

investments Sums of money that are invested in stocks and shares or other financial products

loan A sum of money lent to someone that must be paid back

migrant Moving from place to place

millennium 1,000 years

mural A large painting applied directly to a wall

New Deal, the The measures undertaken by President Roosevelt to overcome the Great Depression

perspective The ability to see different aspects of a problem or issue

plagued Caused continuous trouble

predilection Fondness for or bias toward something

prejudice An opinion for or against something

preserved Kept in its original condition

primary source A firsthand account or direct evidence of an event

renewal Putting new life into something

secondary source Material created by studying primary sources

shantytown A run-down area on the outskirts of a town, with poor houses and shacks, and limited services

share One of the equal parts or shares of a company that allows its holder to gain a share of the company's profits

source Original document or other piece of evidence

source material Evidence of an event in the form of documents, photographs, diaries, and other items

stock market A place where the stocks and shares of companies are bought and sold

stockbroker A person who buys and sells stocks and shares for people

stocks Shares in the ownership and wealth of a company

technology Machinery and equipment made from scientific knowledge

transcript A written version of something spoken

vicissitudes A change for the worse in a situation

visual Something that we see with our eyes

vulnerable Easily hurt or damaged

welfare system A program that gives help to those in need

INDEX